Poems

David Harmer was born in 1952. He lives in South Yorkshire and is married to Paula. They have two piratical daughters, Lizzie and Harriet. David used to swab the decks and walk the plank in a primary school, being the head teacher. He escaped, raised the Jolly Roger, and now sails the mighty oceans of the country as a poet and a drama teacher. He has really enjoyed making all these pirate poems, cramming them full of scurvy sea dogs and nefarious knaves. If you enjoyed the book yell, 'Aye aye, Cap'n!' very loudly wherever and whenever you like. OOH-ARR!

Five facts about **Matt Buckingham**:
- Matt has illustrated many books over the years – his own stories and for other authors
- Matt used to design fire engines until he went to study illustration at Loughborough University and University College Falmouth
- Matt now lives in Staffordshire with his dog, Ben
- Matt likes toast
- Matt plays football at weekends (although he thinks he's better than he really is!)

Also available from Macmillan

HOW TO SURVIVE SCHOOL
Poems chosen by David Harmer

SPILL THE BEANS
Poems by David Harmer and Paul Cookson

THE TRUTH ABOUT PARENTS
Poems by Paul Cookson, David Harmer,
Brian Moses and Roger Stevens

Pirate
Poems

David Harmer

Illustrated by Matt Buckingham

MACMILLAN CHILDREN'S BOOKS

To Sue, one of the brightest, boldest and bravest of them all

First published 2007 by Macmillan Children's Books
a division of Macmillan Publishers Limited
20 New Wharf Road, London N1 9RR
Basingstoke and Oxford
Associated companies throughout the world
www.panmacmillan.com

ISBN 978-0-330-45181-9

3 5 7 9 8 6 4

A CIP catalogue record for this book is available from
the British Library.

Typeset by Tony Fleetwood
Printed and bound in the UK by CPI Mackays, Chatham ME5 8TD

Contents

The First Poem in the Book:
The First Treasure Map

Here be you by yourself
Perusing books upon a shelf.

Here be you with a sigh
Wondering which book to buy.

Here be you with a glance
Giving Davy's book a chance.

Here be me saying 'See!
What a brainy child you be.'

Here be me grinning wide
As you takes a peep inside.

Here be you, as you say
'Not bad this book, it's OK!'

Here be me saying 'Wow!
Hopes you likes it anyhow.'

Here be you thinking 'What
A fantastic book I've got!'

Here be the first page of this book
Full of pirates, take a look.

These Be the Rules

1) The captain is always right.

2) Even when he or she is wrong. See Rule 1 above.

3) All prize money, gold, chewing gum, sweets, doubloons, pieces of eight, nine and ten, pocket money, chocolate bars, mint humbugs and precious jewels to be shared equally.

4) The captain gets ten shares, everyone else gets one.

5) See Rule 1 above. And Rule 2. Or see this cutlass and this pistol pointing at you.

6) No pirate shall say rude things about the captain in front of a parrot. Let the parrot go first. If it dares.

7) All parrots to be properly fed, watered and their mess cleaned up in the crew's quarters. Not near the captain. That's *not* why it's called a poop deck.

8) No spitting, burping, belching, stenching, kicking, nipping, punching, pinching, gouging, gashing, walloping, lashing, thumping, bashing, bumping or trashing when talking/arguing/discussing treasure or any other matter with the captain.

9) See Rule 1 above. And Rule 5. And this musket.

10) All weevils, maggots, bargemen and ship's creepy-crawlies to be shared when times is bad and food is hard to find. Or if the captain fancies a hot bowl of tasty weevil soup.

11) All pirates to practise saying 'Arrrrrrrrrr' and 'Avast there ye lubbers' each day at ten in the morning. Except on Sunday mornings, when the Captain is having a lie-in. See Rule 1 above.

12) Evening classes in swabbing the decks and saying 'Yo-ho-ho' every Thursday.

13) When reaching safe harbour, all pirates may go ashore for two hours only. Before they leave they must wash behind their ears and brush their teeth, comb their beards and trim all nasal hairs with their cutlass. Once ashore, they must not use same cutlass to pick their teeth or their noses. (Use of second, perhaps cleaner, cutlass allowed). They may have a light meal and three glasses of fizzy lemonade before returning to the ship for their bedtime story from the captain.

14) Eyepatches to be worn at all times, even if you don't need one.

15) No mutinies or marooning of the captain allowed. See Rule 1 above.

Blackbeard's Ghost
(As written by Israel Hands, First Mate)

I've seen him many times
like a plume of smoke
drifting over the sea
gold and red in the evening light.

His beard blazes with fire
his pistols explode
as he shoots at the shadows
of scudding clouds.

He turns to me as he always did
fog pouring out of his eyes
a long howl streaming
from his ragged mouth.

He commands me to climb
ropes and rigging to the high crow's-nest
calls 'What d'ye see? What d'ye see?'
his voice as deep as the rolling tide.

'I see nothing,' I tell him
'There is nowhere to climb
there is only the sunset over the islands
stone-white beaches turning to fire.

'I see only a gull
cutting a line through the silent air
and my own face staring
in the rocky pools along the shore.

'And a ghost afloat on the waves
calling out forever
from the caves of death.
That is all I see,' I tell him
'Nothing more.'

The Last Thoughts
of Caleb Jones, Pirate

I can see the gallows
Through the bars
Of my prison cell
They're hanging the stars.

They're hanging the stars
Or so it seems
But they hang me too
In all my dreams.

In all my dreams
I'm filled with fears
Time drifts away
Tomorrow nears.

Tomorrow nears
With heavy tread
Tomorrow morning
They'll see me dead.

They'll see me dead
At the rise of the sun
And all my pirating
Past will be done.

Past will be done
I'll rove no more
Across the oceans
From shore to shore.

From shore to shore
Of the Spanish Main
But listen closely
I'd do it again.

I'd do it again
Wouldn't change a thing
So tomorrow morning
They'll hear me sing.

They'll hear me sing
Of my pirate ways
And I'll smile and smile
As I end my days.

Be You Pirates, Shipmates?

Be you pirates, shipmates?
Ooh-arr, ooh-arr
Be you pirates, shipmates?
Ooh-arr, ooh-arr.

Be you able to join my crew?
Be you able to pirate too?
Be you able to buckle and swash?
Be you able to never wash?

Be you able to swagger and shout?
Be you able to turn about?
Be you able to swab the decks?
Be you able to risk your necks?

Be you pirates, shipmates?
Ooh-arr, ooh-arr
Be you pirates, shipmates?
Ooh-arr, ooh-arr.

Be you able to mark a map?
Be you able to settle a scrap?
Be you able to fly our flag?
Be you able to swipe some swag?

Be you able to rig the sails?
Be you able to sail through gales?
Be you able to hornpipe dance?
Be you able to take a chance?

Be you pirates, shipmates?
Ooh-arr, ooh-arr
Be you pirates, shipmates?
Ooh-arr, ooh-arr.

If you are able to do these things
Then climb aboard and fly with wings
Made of canvas, wood and tar
Guided by the moon and star
Guided by the sun and tide
Far across the oceans wide
We'll ride the sea mile after mile
Until we come to treasure isle
There we'll find our weight in gold
And silver, rubies, pearls I'm told.
Then you'll live the pirate way
Each and every single day
Yes indeed you'll pirates be
So come on, shipmates, sail with me.

Be you pirates, shipmates?
Ooh-arr, ooh-arr
Be you pirates, shipmates?
Ooh-arr, ooh-arr.

Be you able to climb a mast?
Be you able to do it fast?
Be you able to swing your blade?
Be you able to fight and raid?

Be you able to spike a gun?
Be you able to have some fun?
Be you able to chew and spit?
Be you able to do your bit?

Be you pirates, shipmates?
Ooh-arr, ooh-arr
Be you pirates, shipmates?
Ooh-arr, ooh-arr.

Be you able not to blubber?
Be you able to loathe a lubber?
Be you able to row your boat
Be you able on flotsam to float?

Be you able to say 'Jim lad'?
Be you able to be quite bad?
Be you able to sail the sea?
Be you able to sail with me?

Be you pirates, shipmates?
Ooh-arr, ooh-arr
Be you pirates, shipmates?
Ooh-arr, ooh-arr.

Aye you be able to sail the sea
You be able to sail with me.

How To Be a Pirate

First you need a hat
One with three corners or perhaps
One like Nelson wears on his column
But add a skull and crossbones.

Failing that, make one out of paper.

Then you will need a coat
A big, green velvet number
With huge cuffs and gold buttons.

Failing that, an old tracky top will do.

Get some sea boots
Long and leathery, soaked
In salt and the blood of your enemy.

Failing that, try some wellies.

Of course you'll need a parrot
Perched on your shoulder
One that squawks and shouts
'Pieces of eight, pieces of eight.'

*Failing that, get a wooden one
at the toy-shop.*

You need a cutlass
A pistol, some knives
And a blunderbuss
Buy them at the Pirate Store.

Failing that, go back to the toy-shop.

Then you'll have to find a map
Of Broken-Skull Island
In some old sea chest
There's swamps and skeletons
And X marks the spot.

Failing that, draw one in crayon
on some old rolls of wallpaper.

Now you'll need a ship
Three masts full of sail
Three decks full of cannons.

Failing that, try a tree
leafy rigging and ropes of sunlight
or an old table, upside down
with mops for masts.

Set sail at once
Dig up your treasure
Even if it does look a bit
Like Dad's daffodil bulbs
And a handfuls of pebbles.

Failing that, go to the sweet shop
for some chocolate money.

Then practise
Saying 'Yo-ho-ho
Shiver me timbers, I'll slice
Yer gizzards, you scurvy landlubber.'

Failing that, go inside for some tea.

The Pirate Stomp
(To the steady beat of stamping feet)

Yo-ho-ho
Yo-ho-ho
It's a-pirating we go
Yo-ho-ho
Yo-ho-ho
It's a-pirating we go.

I'm Pirate Pete, Pirate Pete
Great big cutlass, stinky feet.

I'm Pirate Trish, Pirate Trish
Want to feed you to the fish.

I'm Pirate Dan, Pirate Dan
Stealing treasure is my plan.

Yo-ho-ho
Yo-ho-ho
It's a-pirating we go
Yo-ho-ho
Yo-ho-ho
It's a-pirating we go.

I'm Pirate Taylor, Pirate Taylor
Pinch your ship and then I'll sail her.

I'm Pirate Ben, Pirate Ben
You'll never see your gold again.

I'm Pirate Jean, Pirate Jean
Hateful, horrid, spiteful, mean.

Yo-ho-ho
Yo-ho-ho
It's a-pirating we go

Yo-ho-ho
Yo-ho-ho
It's a-pirating we go.

I'm the Captain of this crew
Pirating is what we do
Sail across the salty waves
A ghastly group of nasty knaves
We're not pleasant, we're not nice
Steal your treasure in a trice
Then of course we'll steal your ship
So join with us, or take a dip
In the foaming, freezing seas
With an anchor round your knees
Or a stone around your neck
As we dance upon your deck
Shouting, singing, Yo-ho-ho
It's a-pirating we go!

Yo-ho-ho
Yo-ho-ho
It's a-pirating we go
Yo-ho-ho
Yo-ho-ho
It's a-pirating we go.

I'm Pirate Hank, Pirate Hank
You are going to walk my plank.

I'm Pirate Sky, Pirate Sky
You can't escape, don't even try.

I'm Pirate Joe, Pirate Joe
Robbing you – here I go!

Yo-ho-ho
Yo-ho-ho
It's a-pirating we go
Yo-ho-ho
Yo-ho-ho
It's a-pirating we go.

I'm Pirate Clare, Pirate Clare
Have a sword-fight if you dare.

I'm Pirate John, Pirate John
Cut your throat and then I'm gone.

I'm Pirate Mary, Pirate Mary
Like a nightmare, really scary.

Yo-ho-ho
Yo-ho-ho
It's a-pirating we go
Yo-ho-ho
Yo-ho-ho
It's a-pirating we go.

A True Tale (or so they say)

My name is Conanjee Agria
Beware! I am a pirate!
My fleet of ships, many
With more than forty guns,
Rules the coast of India
The Arabian Sea is at my mercy
The eighteenth century lies at my feet
Like a lamb to be slaughtered.

I fall upon the English traders
Like a hungry wolf, my sons and I
Howl like devils as we attack,
Our trusted men show little mercy
To the boats we plunder
Our scimitars are broad and curved
Sharp as a dragon's teeth
Our cannon are fierce and powerful
More fiery than a dragon's flames
Beware! I am a pirate!

We will take your cargo
Your silks and spices, gold and silver
Sending captains of your navy,
Boys still wet from their mother's tears,
Is of no use. We will kill them.
Sending grizzled sea dogs

Who know these waters well
Is of no use. We will kill them.

Leave me to my pirate ways
There is nothing you can do
If you think I am too old
Too slow, weak in my wits
Beware! I am a pirate!
I have such breath in my lungs
Such strength in my limbs
Such amazing light in my eyes.
And when it is my time to die
My son Sunbhajee will take over
Continue to pillage and to rob
From the English ships
There is nothing any one of you can do
Beware! We are pirates!

Pirates on the Playground

Here be the bell, here be the door
Out we run, such uproar!

Here be playtime, yes we're free
Here be the spot where we three be.

Here be me, here be Jane
Here be our mate, Billy Payne.

Here be our yard, a yellow boat
Painted on it, off we float.

Here be our Jolly Roger flying
Here be Jack, why's he crying?

Here be Miriam, here be Paul
Pinched Jack's sweets and ate them all.

Here be me and my crew
We know exactly what to do.

Here be us doing good
Pirates but like Robin Hood.

Here be the spot where we said
'Return Jack's sweets or you are dead.'

Here be the place where things got rough
Just as well Jane's so tough.

Here be the sweets we gave back
Not many left, sorry Jack.

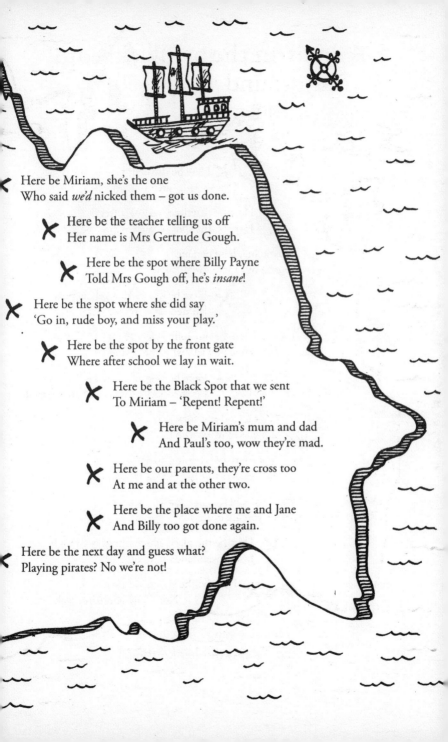

Here be Miriam, she's the one
Who said *we'd* nicked them – got us done.

Here be the teacher telling us off
Her name is Mrs Gertrude Gough.

Here be the spot where Billy Payne
Told Mrs Gough off, he's *insane*!

Here be the spot where she did say
'Go in, rude boy, and miss your play.'

Here be the spot by the front gate
Where after school we lay in wait.

Here be the Black Spot that we sent
To Miriam – 'Repent! Repent!'

Here be Miriam's mum and dad
And Paul's too, wow they're mad.

Here be our parents, they're cross too
At me and at the other two.

Here be the place where me and Jane
And Billy too got done again.

Here be the next day and guess what?
Playing pirates? No we're not!

Babysitting Baby Blackbeard

When Blackbeard was a baby
His ma and pa went out
But little baby Blackbeard
Did not scream or shout
His grandpa and his granny
Both came babysitting
Grandpa cleaned his cutlass
And Granny did her knitting.

They carried on quite calmly
Until the baby woke
Grandpa now was fast asleep
So for a little joke
Blackbeard tied the laces
Of his sea boots together
Climbed the curtain like some rigging
Feeling very clever.

'Ship Ahoy!' the baby cried
Grandpa shouted 'What?'
And 'Where?' and 'Why?' and 'When?'
And then 'What treasure has it got?'
But as he stood, down he fell
His timbers were all shivered
Baby Blackbeard laughed like mad
And like a jelly quivered.

'Come down right now,' his granny said
'It's time you had your shave.'
She poked his bottom with her cutlass
Just so he would behave
But no, he swarmed along the pole
Towards the other curtain
Which made them spit and shout and swear
Of that you can be certain.

Grandpa had spent his life
Climbing to the crow's-nest
So clambering up ropes and poles
Was what he did the best
It wasn't long before he'd got
Young Blackbeard by the nappy
He pulled and tugged and heaved and hauled
And caught the naughty chappie.

The baby was a bit upset
And he pulled out his gun
Which was a proper blunderbuss
Not one you'd buy for fun
But his granny soothed him
Gave him a gold doubloon
And said 'Now choose a neighbour
You might like to maroon.'

So at last his granny shaved
The whiskers from his face
And after pistol practice
At which he was an ace
They got little Blackbeard
In his cot to settle
Then thought they'd have a cup of tea
And put on the kettle.

So baby Blackbeard snored and snored
Content throughout the night
And when his ma and pa returned
In early morning light
They asked if he had been quite good
A perfect little star?
'Of course he was,' said Granny
'Perfect,' said Grandpa.

Twelve Ways to Spot
a Pirate in Disguise

1) A peg leg peeping
   From the bottom of his jeans.

2) He might *look* like your head teacher
   He might *shout* like your head teacher
   He might *dress* like your head teacher
   But he still says 'Ah-harrrrrr'
   And calls you 'Jim lad'.

3) Who are all those people
   Covered in long coats
   Waiting outside the pet shop
   Under a sign saying 'Cut-Price Parrots'?

4) Some people have a car on the drive
   Some people have a caravan on the drive
   But not many people
   Have a three-masted sloop with cannon
   On the drive.

5) Most policemen
   Don't wear a three-cornered hat with a feather
   Instead of a helmet.

6) You've got an England football flag
   In your window, next door
   They've got a Jolly Roger.

7) Is there a house on your street
   Called 'Dunpirating'?

8) On the shelves
   In the school library
   Are there only copies
   Of *Treasure Island*?

9) When you buy some sweets
    At the corner shop
    Do you get your change
    In pieces of eight?

10) Is the postman
    Wearing a long cutlass
    As well as his postbag?

11) Does the lollipop lady
    Leave you marooned
    On a traffic island?

12) Look hard at your teacher
    Does he or she have
    A large tattoo saying
    'I loves to be a pirate'?

An Extremely Silly and Fairly Meaningless Chant for Two Large Groups of People to Shout Out as Loudly as Possible in a Fierce and Piratical Manner

We are the pirates	*(We are the pirates)*
Jolly jolly pirates	*(Jolly jolly pirates)*
And when they ask us	*(And when they ask us)*
Where do we come from?	*(Where do we come from?)*
We'll tell them we're the pirates	*(We'll tell them we're the pirates)*
Jolly jolly pirates	*(Jolly jolly pirates)*
I am Lucinda	*(Her name's Lucinda)*
I'm a jolly pirate	*(She's a jolly pirate)*
I've got a pistol	*(She's got a pistol)*
But it only fires water	*(It only fires water)*
My name is Debbie	*(Her name is Debbie)*
I'm a jolly pirate	*(She's a jolly pirate)*
I've got a cutlass	*(She's got a cutlass)*
It's only made of plastic	*(It's only made of plastic)*
I am Joshua	*(His name is Joshua)*
I'm a jolly pirate	*(He's a jolly pirate)*
I've got an eyepatch	*(He's got an eyepatch)*
It's only made of paper	*(It's only made of paper)*

My name is Iqbal   *(His name is Iqbal)*
I'm a jolly pirate   *(He's a jolly pirate)*
I've got a treasure map   *(He's got a treasure map)*
I drew it in my bedroom   *(He drew it in his bedroom)*

I am Mae-Ling   *(Her name is Mae-Ling)*
I'm a jolly pirate   *(She's a jolly pirate)*
I've got a headscarf   *(She's got a headscarf)*
And great big earrings   *(And great big earrings)*

My name is Javed   *(His name is Javed)*
I'm a jolly pirate   *(He's a jolly pirate)*
I've got a parrot   *(He's got a parrot)*
It's made of cardboard   *(It's made of cardboard)*

We are the pirates   *(We are the pirates)*
Jolly jolly pirates   *(Jolly jolly pirates)*
And when they ask us   *(And when they ask us)*
Where do we come from?   *(Where do we come from?)*
We'll tell them we're   *(We'll tell them we're*
  the pirates   *the pirates)*
Jolly jolly pirates   *(Jolly jolly pirates)*

The Old Sea Dog

You can always find me here by the fire
a quiet corner of the Jolly Hangman
and I'll sing my old songs of lost pirate days
when our gallant ship sailed
through gales and ice, through burning sun
salt stinging our eyes like tears.

The young men laugh, don't believe me
when I talk of my fight with Barbary Jack
or blazing my pistols at Diamond Annie
swinging my cutlass at Gunpowder Billy.

Then I tell them of hunting our quarry
our proud skull and crossbones high in the mast
our victim's ship clear in the spyglass
we'd bind ourselves to them with great hooks
and then my crew of villainous pirates
dreams of treasure burning holes in their hearts
swarmed over their decks like rats in a barrel
sucking the life out of their eyes.

The young men stop laughing
when I speak of the time
I slit the throat of Black-Hearted Evans
saw him tumble and spin like a broken wheel
into the mouth of the raging waters.

Their faces go pale when I draw this blade
their laughter dies as quickly as he did
that cold autumn morning so long ago
and just like the rest of his scurvy crew
the young men run
leaving me with my memories
flooding through me like the rising tide.

Who Will Sail with Davy Jones?

(Davy Jones is the ghostly, underwater pirate who claims the souls of sailors drowned at sea and shuts them away in his sea chest or locker.)

If bony Davy calls your name
Your soul and body he will claim
In his domain you'll gain your fame
And hear his dismal tones
'Come sail along with Davy Jones'.

And we have had some narrow squeaks
So many ships have sprung with leaks
Our names are what old Davy seeks
When his dark music drones
'Come sail along with Davy Jones'.

Our first ship, the *London Town*
Was quick and fast, of great renown
A Spanish schooner shot her down
She sank like a sack of stones
'Come sail along with Davy Jones'.

Our next ship, a nippy clipper
Along the Eastern seas we'd slip her
But she was sunk by a Swedish skipper
Just like a bag of bones
'Come sail along with Davy Jones'.

Next we took an American schooner
Stars and Stripes, the *Brave Altoona*
But a Scottish pirate said he'd 'droon' her
Out in the tropical zones
'*Come sail along with Davy Jones*'.

We filched a frigate, the *Rising Sun*
But a coastguard hit her with his gun
She filled with water, we had to run
We heard her timbers' groans
'Come sail along with Davy Jones'.

Now we have a splendid ship
Three decks with cannon every trip
We won't ever lose our grip
And drown with horrid moans
'Come sail along with Davy Jones'.

So if old Davy calls her name
We'll tell him 'No, oh what a shame!'
And carry on our pirate game
Anonymous unknowns
We will not sail with Davy Jones.

How Pirate Jane Grabbed All the Buried Treasure of Spyglass Island

Here be the spot where Pirate Jane
Said 'Let's have my chicken soup again!'

Here be the spot where the crew
Guzzled down that dodgy stew.

Here be the spot where Pirate Bill
Suddenly was very ill.

Here be the spot where Pirate Jack
Had a bilious attack.

Here be the spot where Pirate Jake
Had a violent stomach ache.

Here be the spot where Pirate Rick
Suddenly was very sick.

Here be the spot where Pirate Paul
Was the sickest of them all.

Here be the spot where Pirate Dawn
Had a technicolour yawn.

Here be the spot where Pirate Sue
Knew she'd been poisoned by that stew.

Here be the spot where Pirate Lee
Had to dive behind a tree.

Here be the spot where Pirate Kate
Brought up everything she ate.

Here be the spot where
Pirate Jane
Grabbed the treasure,
went home by plane.

Maybe One Day

When I grow up
I'm going to be a pirate
I've seen Johnny Depp
He will inspire it
I'll shout and swagger
Sail across the sea
Then Keira Knightley
Will want to snog me.

A Difficult Day at
the Cuttlefish Cafe

There was a fierce pirate
in Weston-super-Mare
who packed in all his pirating
because he did not care
for reckless buccaneering
with a cut-throat crew
he dropped his anchor, came ashore
and knew just what to do
he started a tea-shop
with cuppas, ices, cakes
beans on toast, fish and chips
scones and thick milkshakes

he settled there quite happily
with daughter, son and wife
sold his parrot and his gun
left his pirate life.

But one day a coach trip
of pirates out for fun
came to Weston-super-Mare
for a spot of sun
they built castles on the beach
and paddled in the sea
and then they all felt thirsty
and wanted cups of tea
they rattled all their cutlasses
yelled and danced about
but fell completely silent
when their pirate friend came out.

'Well shiver all me timbers!'
cried one brave pirate lad
'It's Crazy Cut-Throat Cuttlefish
the baddest of the bad
we heard that you were drownded
lost at sea somewhere
but now we find you serving tea
in Weston-super-Mare
come along with us my boy
join our next treasure trip
we need a bold bad bloke like you
as captain of our ship.'

The cafe-owning pirate
shook his head and sighed
'I can't sail a silly boat
in fact I've never tried
I'm not the chap you think I am
I've never been to sea
now do you gentlemen require
jam doughnuts with your tea?'

'If you're not him,' said one old salt
through his tangled beard
'Then you're his twin and no mistake
I calls that downright weird.'
'The chocolate buns are very good,'
said Cut-Throat Cuttlefish
'You'll like the strawberry ice cream
we sell it by the dish.'

The pirates all were curious
they knew they had their man
so they grabbed him by the throat
that's when the fun began
he seized them by their jackets
he seized them by their hair
one minute they were drinking tea
and the next they were not there
lying in the gutter
they heard him give a shout
'You scurvy swabs and lubbers
all of you GET OUT!'

When they'd gone his wife said
'My dear I do agree
no pirate life, a quiet life
will do for you and me
let us both just carry on
and live without a care
selling tea and scones with jam
in Weston-super-Mare.'

A Pirate Song

Oh the pirate life is a fine life
Fearless, fair and free
Yes the pirate life is a wild life
And it's the life for me.

I cast my net around the world
Gathered up my crew
Rapscallions and ruffians
Thieves and cut-throats too
I built my ship of English oak
Stole these Spanish sails
Set off to find my fortune through
Tempests, storms and gales.

We sailed across the salty seas
Jolly, brave and bold
Filled up a thousand treasure chests
With rubies, pearls and gold
Diamonds, sapphires, amethysts,
Emeralds and plate
Doubloons and silver guineas
Piles of pieces of eight.

Oh the pirate life is a fine life
Fearless, fair and free
Yes the pirate life is a wild life
And it's the life for me.

As sunrise spread across the waves
So our flags did fly
Our Jolly Roger soaked the blood
From the eastern sky
We soaked our knives and cutlasses
In the blood of men
They walked our plank, they were marooned
Were never seen again.

We caught a thousand other ships
Kept them for the prize
The coins and gold kept rolling in
Right before our eyes
We'd spend it all, we'd spend it well
Then we'd sail again

Head off for the distant waters
Of the Spanish Main.

Oh the pirate life is a fine life
Fearless, fair and free
Yes the pirate life is a wild life
And it's the life for me.

Sometimes we'd fight to stay alive
Or we chose to hide
Up a hidden, narrow creek
On the ebbing tide
Then out we'd roar like dragon's fire
At some merchant craft
Take all her gold, her goods, her crew
As they wept we laughed.

Perhaps we'd bury treasure deep
On some silent shore
And after a twelvemonth had passed
And then another four
Returned to dig it up again
Spend it at our ease
But once it went, when it was spent
We took to the seas.

Oh the pirate life is a fine life
Fearless, fair and free
Yes the pirate life is a wild life
And it's the life for me.

One day a ship pushed through the fog
Close to Boston Sound
We jumped aboard all pirate-like
No crew could be found
We searched that ship from stern to bow
Then from bow to stern
No sailors, but her sails were trimmed
And her wheel did turn.

Then suddenly around us all
Appeared a ragged band
Of skeletons and misty wraiths
Fighting hand to hand
We had to scream, we had to cry
What dread ship sails these coasts?
It was the *Flying Dutchman*
And we were fighting ghosts.

Oh the pirate life is a fine life
Fearless, fair and free
Yes the pirate life is a wild life
And it's the life for me.

On ropes we swung back to our ship
From those phantoms fled
It's hard enough to fight the living
Never mind the dead
We set our course for Africa
A safer place by far
And robbed a fine, fat galleon
Just off Zanzibar.

Year in, year out we pirated
Famous buccaneers
Brought terror to the shipping lanes
Stirred the wildest fears
We knew each day that we might die
From hanging or the knife
But never ever did we try
To quit our pirate life.

Oh the pirate life is a fine life
Fearless, fair and free
Yes the pirate life is a wild life
And it's the life for me.

We came across another ship
In Jamaica Bay
It seemed a simple, easy strike
Lightning-like you'd say
But just as we all climbed aboard
We walked into a trap
And from the shore a cannon roared
Like a thunderclap.

And from the hold armed soldiers came
Intent upon our end
We fought them hard and long and well
And many did we send
Into the arms of Davy Jones
For one last bony dance
And once at last we'd all escaped
We set sail for France.

Oh the pirate life is a fine life
Fearless, fair and free
Yes the pirate life is a wild life
And it's the life for me.

But sometimes as I sniff the air
Breathe in salt and spray
I feel the deck beneath my feet
I feel the pitch and sway
Of our fine ship the *Brave Marie*
As she flies along
The many paths we pirates took
And I sing my song.

My sleep is stuffed with pirate dreams
From times so long ago
I miss the voices, miss the talk
Mates I used to know
But even in my sleep I sail
Clear to Barbary
I sing my song and I recall
What it meant to me.

Oh the pirate life is a fine life
Fearless, fair and free
Yes the pirate life is a wild life
And it's the life for me.

Scarface Moore

*(Believe it or not, my dreaded old head teacher
had a piratical ancestor.)*

Scarface Moore
Scarface Moore
Kicking in my cabin door
Crack – smash
Crack crack smash
Crack – smash
Crack crack smash

Scarface Moore's got a pistol that shoots
Scarface Moore's got big sea boots
Scarface Moore's the terror of the sea
And Scarface Moore is after me!

Scarface Moore
Scarface Moore
Kicking in my cabin door
Crack – smash
Crack crack smash
Crack – smash
Crack crack smash

Yesterday when we sailed away
I felt OK, till he chased and caught us
Now Scarface Moore's outside my door
Wants to slice me with his cutlass!

Scarface Moore
Scarface Moore
Kicking in my cabin door
Crack – smash
Crack crack smash
Crack – smash
Crack crack smash

Oh, Scarface Moore, I implore
Don't kick down my cabin door
Find me shaking on the floor
Grabbing me with your claw
Nicking my treasure from my drawer
Leaving me skint and poor
Just to settle up the score
Just because last time I swore
I'd cut your nose off, Scarface Moore.

Scarface Moore
Scarface Moore
Kicking in my cabin door
Crack – smash
Crack crack smash
Crack – smash
Crack crack smash

I'm through the window, down the side
Of our ship, there's the longboat
I'm rowing free, no need to hide
I've escaped that deadly cut-throat.

Scarface Moore
Scarface Moore
Kicking in my cabin door
Crack – smash
Crack crack smash
Crack – smash
Crack crack smash

Scarface Moore's got a pistol that shoots
Scarface Moore's got big sea boots
Scarface Moore's the terror of the sea
And Scarface Moore is after me!

Scarface Moore
Scarface Moore
Kicking my cabin door
Crack – smash
Crack crack smash
Crack – smash
Crack crack smash

Is Our Teacher a Secret Pirate?

Each day he wore the same grey suit
the same grey shirt, grey tie, grey socks
the same grey shoes, grey overcoat
the same grey seaside for his holidays
but this year something's happened
Mr Jones has changed.

He's grown a great bushy beard
he wears a huge golden earring
a spotted hanky on his head
a striped shirt and big black boots
a parrot that swears on his shoulder
an anchor that's tattooed on his arm.

In geography we study maps of islands
in maths we count gold doubloons
in science we look at skeletons
in PE we swing from ropes
in art lessons we draw black flags
with a skull and crossbones on the front.

Yesterday
he dug up the Infants' sandpit
pulled out a heavy wooden chest
and shouted 'Blistering barnacles'.

But today he's vanished
no one knows where he is
so now we have another teacher
one we've never met before
Mr Silver.

Pirate's Dawn

Mist seeps across the sea
red-hot needles of early light
pierce our sails
beneath my feet
the ship shifts its weight
aching at anchor, impatient
for the day to cut its iron chains
send it skimming over the ocean
like a giant bird.

The morning's breeze lifts the mist
and a faint smell of charcoal
gunpowder and blood
drifts in with the tide
I watch the bodies dip and bob
near the beach by the rocks
the gash in my forehead stinging
in the fresh, salt winds
and the dawn's first gull
sweeps through the air, crying
a drowned mariner seeking comfort.

Yesterday's battle is over
the navy came for us
their guns blistered our skin with venom
we cut and stabbed and fired our cannon
blew great holes in their decks

swarmed aboard with our axes
felled their forests of masts
they tumbled and crashed
in a riot of rigging
sailcloth and sailors tangled and broken
those who could swim escaped our pistols
the others float just over there
as if they might wake, strike out for the shore.

Now the sun gleams like a gold doubloon
the sky is clear, our sails are stirring
soon we shall slip away from here
into tomorrow.

The Famous Last Words of Some Very Unlucky Pirates

What cannonball?   *Black Jack Jones*

I bet that pistol ain't even loaded!   *Mad Matilda McGrew*

No, you scurvy mutineers
I'm the captain of this ship!   *Cut-Throat Carver*

Aaaaaaaaaaaaaaaagh!   *Deadly Dawkins*

Indoor Pirates

Our pirate craft *Crazy Mabel*
Made from boxes and a table

Our deadly enemies Smigsy's lot
On their ship the *Black Spot*.

We land on a rocky shore
Smigsy shouts 'This means war!'

We climb steep cliffs, well the stairs
Fight hand to hand, and Smigsy dares

To swing one-handed from a shelf
Brings it crashing on himself!

Here be dragons, here be fuss
Mum is really furious.

There's more trouble by this tree
Smigsy's gone and cut his knee.

Mum sticks a plaster on his scrape
He's our prisoner, no escape.

His crew are brave, they fight on
But Smigsy says 'All right, you've won.'

But right now it's time to stop
And eat some crisps, drink some pop.

Yes it's really time for tea
The war is over now you see.

We've won the treasure, Yo-ho-ho
Tomorrow we'll have another go.

The Crew of the *Crazy Mabel*: Me (aged 9), my sister Chloe (7) and my brother Charlie (7)
The Crew of the *Black Spot*: Smigsy (aged 9), his sister Annie (8) and his brother Ben (7)

The One They Feared the Most

Morgan made them walk the plank
Ann Bonnie danced on dead men's bones
Bonnet flew the Jolly Roger
Rackham sailed with Davy Jones.

William Fly hanged them high
Crazy Mary sank them fast
Edmund Low stole their gold
Thomas Tew smashed their mast.

Moody blew their boats to bits
Rackham set their sails on fire
Kennedy cut off their ears
Cutlass Liz was vile and dire.

But the one they feared the most
Was Old Blackbeard, Edward Teach
He taught them all the dance of death
On their final, rocky beach.

Ben Gunn's Blues

(In Treasure Island *by R. L. Stevenson, Jim Hawkins and his friends find Ben Gunn marooned by Captain Flint on the island. Ben asks if they have any toasted cheese.)*

I'm poor Ben Gunn, a hungry man
Very partial to Parmesan
Tell me young sir, tell me please
Have you any toasted cheese?

Flint had a heart as stern as stone
Marooned poor Ben to die alone
You have come and saved my skin
But look at the starving state I'm in.

I need to feed but my dream is clear
No bacon, eggs or spuds, no fear
What I need most, I hopes you agrees
Is heaps and heaps of toasted cheese.

Cheddar, Lymeswold, Edam or Blue
Stilton, Gouda, Lancashire too,
Roast it, toast it, lovely stuff
Give me some now, I can't get enough.

I won't eat cold cheese at any price
You can feed it to the mice
You know what I want, I'm on my knees
I must have a slice of toasted cheese.

I'll show you exactly what cunning Ben did
Dug up Flint's treasure, I've got it hid
In the dark caves along by the shore
That's it for now, I'll say no more.

But if you want gold, here's the deal
Great chunks of cheese for my next meal
Take all the treasure away at your ease
As Ben Gunn feasts on his toasted cheese.

A Pirate Shanty

Blow hard winds, blow well
Blow lustily, propel
Our pirate ship through pirate dreams
Piratical plans, piratical schemes
Until we hear the knell
Of the cracked black bells of hell.

Tobago, Jamaica, Cadiz
Bristol, New England, Peru
North Carolina, South Carolina
Chile and Florida too.

Trinidad, Boston, New York
London, Newcastle, Spain
Canada, Falmouth, then Labrador
Risk rounding Cape Horn once again.

Plymouth, the Cape of Good Hope
Past Iceland, Greenland, Biscay
The sea of monsoons, the sea of no winds
Ploughing the salty way.

Chasing the trade winds to where
The lightning dances like fire
Around our topgallants and mizzenmast too
Bright blue and it's true I'm no liar.

Blow hard winds, blow well
Blow lustily, propel
Our pirate ship through pirate dreams
Piratical plans, piratical schemes
Until we hear the knell
Of the cracked black bells of hell.

Mumbai, Japan, Finisterre
Tierra del Fuego and Cuba
The grey English Channel, far Panama
Glasgow, Dublin, Vancouver.

Around the whole world in three years
Circumnavigate there and the best
The tropics of Cancer and Capricorn
And never, not ever, find rest.

One day we know it will end
As we fly across the Equator
The Royal Navy barks at our heels
They'll catch us sooner or later.

But today we are bound for the East
China and then Singapore
The Straits of Cathay call us on our way
Farewell till you see us once more.

Blow hard winds, blow well
Blow lustily, propel
Our pirate ship through pirate dreams
Piratical plans, piratical schemes
Until we hear the knell
Of the cracked black bells of hell.

Aye, until we hear the knell
Of the cracked black bells of hell.

The Powder Monkey's Tale

(Powder monkeys were young boys who had the job of carrying gunpowder to the cannons in the heat of a battle.)

Look after the powder monkey, make sure he survives
Look after the powder monkey, he will save your lives.

My name is Jacob and I'm a powder monkey
Only ten years old but I'm stocky and I'm chunky
Swinging through the jungle of all these masts and rigging
Dodging all the hellfire, zagging and a-zigging.

My eyes are streaming, stinging and a-weeping
With gunpowder in my sack I come a-leaping
Shot and bullets all around, empty muzzles smoking
It's foggy and it's smoggy, I'm already choking.

Look after the powder monkey, make sure he survives
Look after the powder monkey, he will save your lives.

Cannonballs hot and fierce past my ears are screaming
Bodies fall to the deck, a nightmare I'm dreaming
The ship's timbers smash, a spear attack of splinters
Death's grip on my mates is colder than the winter's.

Then I see our captain's ammunition is expended
Our enemy's at his throat, his life is nearly ended
He shouts at me right out loud, speaking very thickly
'Ship ahoy! Where's that boy! Get me powder quickly!'

Look after the powder monkey, make sure he survives
Look after the powder monkey, he will save your lives.

He yells at me once again and I go a-scurrying
To the munitions store I go a-hurrying
I fetch what he needs, he carries on his fighting
And before too long, victory he's sighting.

We fire another broadside and then start cheering
The noise and din are so loud it's stealing my hearing
Grappling irons fly like snakes, iron teeth a-gripping
Come on lads, here we go, into the foe we're ripping.

Look after the powder monkey, make sure he survives
Look after the powder monkey, he will save your lives.

Pretty soon they give up, our captain cries 'Surrender
But don't be blue, join my crew, that is my agenda!
Let's sell your ship, grab your gold and all your booty
Split it up between us all, what a pleasant duty.'

They all cheer, yell out loud, glad to stop the drubbing
I go back to my work, swabbing and a-scrubbing
But the captain intervenes when he sees me frowning
Yells 'But for Jacob here, we'd all be drowning!'

Look after the powder monkey, make sure he survives
Look after the powder monkey, he will save your lives.

'Let's thank the powder monkey, he's a splendid fellow.'
He tosses me a guinea coin, bright and gold and yellow
Then that is that, he turns his back, off we go a-sailing
But I am glowing full of pride here beside this railing.

Yes, my name is Jacob and I'm a powder monkey
Only ten years old but I'm stocky and I'm chunky
All this tale is true, it happened just today
So now if you'll forgive me, I'll be on my way.

Look after the powder monkey, make sure he survives
Look after the powder monkey, he will save your lives.

Pirate Perkins, Being Completely Skint, Penniless and Poor, but Having His Own White Beard and Being of Large Girth (in other words tubby) Finds a Most Suitable Christmas Job

All day he'd say *Yo-ho-ho*
In carefree pirate banter
Cut off the *Yo* stick to *Ho-ho*
You sound a lot like Santa.

A seaside store as you may know
Gave him a job instanter
Said *Off you go to the grotto*
This year you're playing Santa.

Perkins really stole the show
A wish-for-Christmas granter
Pinching prezzies? Oh no no
He gave them out, like Santa.

Pirate's Moon

Pirate's moon
Blood red, thin clouds
Cut across its face
Like scars in the sky.

Pirate's moon
The shapes of ships
Carved in grey rock
Sail its surface.

Pirate's moon
Fades into white
Swings like a gibbet
On a hook of ice.

Pirate's moon
Lowers its bright lamp
Lights a watery path
Over the harbour.

Pirate's moon
Promising tomorrow
In a silent whisper
Of secret breath.

Pirate's moon
Sighs in our sails
They shiver, tremble
Reach out for the dawn.

The Pirate Queen
of the China Seas

Lai Choi San, queen of the China seas
Lai Choi San, impossible to please
Splendid in satin, gold and jade
Waiting for ransoms to be paid
Her prisoners writhing in their ropes
She smiles like a snake, dashes their hopes
Of rescue and home, she must be obeyed
Nobody leaves until she's been paid,
Lai Choi San, queen of the China seas
Lai Choi San, impossible to please.

Lai Choi San, giving her enemies heat
Lai Choi San, twelve boats sail in her fleet
Each one has a cannon ready to blast
The sails away from an enemy's mast
And then she captures her victim's gold
And most of the crew into slavery sold
Save for the officers as I've just said
Sold for high ransoms, or left for dead,
Lai Choi San, giving her enemies heat
Lai Choi San, twelve boats sail in her fleet.

Lai Choi San, beautiful with black hair
Lai Choi San, defy her if you dare
As tall as a man, as strong as an ox
A biter, a fighter, breaking down locks

Of boxes of treasure, of cases of wine
Stealing their spices, their silk cloth so fine
She rules all the waters along this cold coast
No one defeats her, that's her proud boast,
Lai Choi San, beautiful with black hair
Lai Choi San, defy her if you dare.

A Doubloon for the Sea Cook's Son

(A doubloon being a gold coin but also a poem where two crews shout most things twice, so they double the poem. They can talk all at once or take turns. You work it out for yourself, you scurvy lubbers! OOH-ARR.)

Crew One: Me Hearties

Long John Silver, pirate cook
Long John Silver, pirate, crook
Long John Silver, pirate bold
Long John Silver, stole the gold.

OOH-ARR me hearties
OOH-ARR me hearties
OOH-ARR me hearties
OOH-ARR me hearties

I'm first mate, I'm first rate
I get paid in pieces of eight.

Captain Keith, Captain Keith
Never ever brushed his teeth.

Captain Cox, Captain Cox
Never ever changed his socks.

Crew Two: Me Shipmates

OOH-ARR me shipmates
OOH-ARR me shipmates
OOH-ARR me shipmates
OOH-ARR me shipmates

Long John Silver, wicked man
Long John Silver, wicked plan
Long John Silver so I'm told
Long John Silver stole the gold.

Captain Kidd, Captain Kidd
Sold his granny for a quid.

Captain Farrell, Captain Farrell
Was round and fat, like a barrel.

I'm first mate, I'm first rate
I get paid in pieces of eight.

I'm first mate, I'm first rate (x 2)

I get paid in pieces of eight. (x 2)

BOTH CREWS   We are pirates, just watch out
We are pirates, have no doubt
We are pirates, give you nowt
We are pirates, hear us shout

WE – ARE – PIRATES (x 2)

Lizzie, the Pirate's Young Daughter

Lizzie,* the pirate's young daughter
Was thrown by her dad in the water
It soon came to him
That she couldn't swim
And he thought 'I oughta have taught her.'

*The pirate known as Lizzie Harmer wants ye all to know that she wrote quite a bit of this here limerick. Ooh-arr.

Harriet, a Captain-Type Pirate

Harriet,* a captain-type pirate
Picked up her pistol to fire it
She said 'I'm inciting
No mischief, no fighting
It's just that my pirates require it.'

*The pirate known as Harrier Harmer wants ye all to know that she is actually an admiral. Ooh-arr.

There Once Was a Pirate

There once was a pirate named Peter
Who fought a fierce rival called Rita
Although she was tough
It wasn't enough
And Rita let Peter defeat her.

A foolish young pirate named Simpkin
Shot a hole in his ship without thinking
As the water poured in
Right up to his chin
He said 'I'm not shrinking but sinking!'

There once was a pirate from Preston
Who continually kept his old vest on
His said to his crew
'This old one will do
Cos I can't let my best one get messed on.'

There was a young pirate from Stoke
Who was penniless, totally broke
Then he dreamed with great pleasure
Of digging up treasure
But he spent it before he awoke.

A pirate who sailed to Bermuda
Was bitten by a barracuda
He held up his thumb
Said 'It's bitten my HAND
Otherwise this last line would be ruder.'

The Weevil* and the Very Hungry Pirates

A weevil was trapped inside a ship's biscuit
He stuck out his head and said 'Yes I'll risk it.
I can't hear a knock, or a tap, or a sound
Of some hungry pirate hanging around.'

So out he scuttled and took a quick look
Of what was around him and there stood the cook
Watching him crawl across his big table
And saying 'Well, well, now if I'm able
I'm going to capture this fine piece of meat
Looking so juicy and tasty and sweet
Pop it into the stew to add to the flavour
Then my good cooking the crew will all savour.'

So that's what he did and that's why they got
Plump roasted beetle in their hotpot.

*Weevils were small beetles living in
the hard biscuits, or hardtack, sailors
ate. The pirates would knock their
biscuits first on the table to dislodge
them. In this case the weevil beat them
to it. Also, weevils didn't usually talk.

The Perfectly Pathetic
Pants-at-Being-a-Pirate
Pirate Poem

I'm a pants pirate, boo-hoo-hoo
Not very good at what I do.
I'm a pants pirate, fair enough?
Not very good at pirate stuff.

I've got an eyepatch and I've got
A cutlass on my hip
The only thing I haven't got
Is a pirate ship
I try my best to be a pirate
Fierce as you like
But it's hard to be convincing
When you've only got a bike.

I'm a pants pirate, boo-hoo-hoo
Not very good at what I do.
I'm a pants pirate, fair enough?
Not very good at pirate stuff.

I'm always yelling pirate yells
Like 'Ooh-arr ooh-arr'
But if somebody hears them
They don't run very far
I've tried to get a parrot

Haven't had much luck
The only thing I could find
Was this yellow, plastic duck.

I'm a pants pirate, boo-hoo-hoo
Not very good at what I do.
I'm a pants pirate, fair enough?
Not very good at pirate stuff.

I thought I'd pinch some treasure
From the jewellers in the town
But then I got a puncture
My tyres let me down
I saw a little baby
In a supermarket trolley
Tried to pinch his sweeties
His mum hit me with her brolly.

I'm a pants pirate, boo-hoo-hoo
Not very good at what I do.
I'm a pants pirate, fair enough?
Not very good at pirate stuff.

I've tried so many ways
To own a pirate craft
A canoe with a leak or two
A lilo and a raft
Even bought a rubber dinghy
The kind that you inflate
Straight away I sank it
Being rather overweight.

I'm a pants pirate, boo-hoo-hoo
Not very good at what I do.
I'm a pants pirate, fair enough?
Not very good at pirate stuff.

Perhaps I should give it up
At pirating I'm bad
I try and try and try and try
End up feeling sad
But I suppose I must have
One last final go
So out of the way you scurvy swabs
Yo-ho-ho-ho-ho.*

I'm a pants pirate, boo-hoo-hoo
Not very good at what I do.
I'm a pants pirate, fair enough?
Not very good at pirate stuff.

Sounds more like Father Christmas than a pirate. Like I said, I'm pants at this.

Twelve Ways To Make a Pirate Irate

1) Pinch his treasure map
   Keep all his gold.

2) Make him get up for breakfast
   At seven in the morning
   When he's on holiday.

3) Swap his prize parrot
   For a stuffed pigeon.

4) Make *him* walk the plank.

5) Set fire to his beard
   And his peg leg.

6) Change his tot of rum
   For fizzy pop.

7) Draw a moustache
   And some joke glasses
   On his skull-and-crossbones flag.

8) Swap his deadly flintlocks
   For water pistols.

9) Steal his ship
   Leave him with a leaky canoe
   With no paddles.

10) Whilst he is asleep
Write 'I love my mummy' on his forehead
In purple marker pen.

11) Wash out the swash from his buckles.
Dye his best shirt bright candy pink.

12) Tell everyone
He isn't called Mad Dog McCreadie
But is really Colin Cucumber-Parsley-Hogfeatures-
Wettypoo.
Who wears red-spotted pants.

Calico Kate and her Cut-Throat Crew

Kate was a pirate
Daring and strong
Sailed all the oceans
From here to Hong Kong.

Her crew all adored her
And followed her where
No other pirate crew
Would ever dare.

Perilous Paula
Was Katy's First Mate
Kept everything orderly
Shipshape and straight.

Molly McGuire
Carried five knives
A belt full of pistols
She never spared lives.

Then came Saucy Sue
A brave Yorkshire lass
Aloft in the crow's-nest
With her spyglass.

Wild Wendy from Wakefield
Lynda the Bold
They wore all the diamonds
Sold all the gold.

Lizzie and Harriet
Janet and Jane
Counted the treasure
Again and again.

Lesley the Lucky
And Long Linda-Lee
Fired all the cannon
And made all the tea.

In typhoons and whirlwinds
Ice storms and gales
Whatever the weather
Kate raised her sails.

She raided Jamaica
Attacked Trinidad
She was reckless and fearless
Murderous, mad.

She marauded near Malta
Stormed down the coast
Of Northern America
It was her boast.

That Calico Kate
And her cut-throat crew
Were the wildest pirates
The world ever knew.

And do you know what?
I think that it's true
Do you know what?
I really do!

Grumpy Pirates

After a while
the pirates started to quarrel
about who should have
which bit of treasure.

They had travelled for days
through swamps and jungles
leaving their longboat
scraped up on the shingle
and their ship the *Corsair*
afloat in the bay.

The steaming sun
soaked through their shirts
sweat stung their eyes
it was too hot to argue
but that's what they did
about the doubloons
the gold moidores
the silver shillings
and the shower of guineas
scattered over the rocks.

It was turning nasty
with cutlasses drawn
and pistols pointing
voices were raised.

The youngest pirate started to cry
he was six and sick
of being ignored
the ship's first mate
said it was silly
to keep falling out
but the pirate captain,
his big sister,
said the treasure was hers.
Yeah, so there, whatever!

Just then their mum
called them inside for tea
before a mutiny could erupt
so the pirates sailed
back down the garden
and into the harbour
for beans on toast
and later that evening
the pirates shared
the best pot of making-up chocolate
ever found on the Seven Seas.

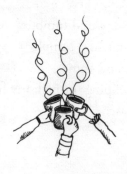

The Very Last Pirate's
Very Last Poem

It's finished now
all over, the pirate life
has gone

like moonlight on the water
dazzling, enticing, alluring

but suddenly
snuffed out like a candle.

All done with now
distorted, dimmed
by a tide of time
by a gale of minutes
by a hurricane of hours
by a whirlwind of years

by a shipwreck of memories
white sands and coral
brave ships and tumbling seas
confusion and tumult
smoke and flame
gold slipping through my fingers
like water.

The sun is setting
I look through my spyglass

not a sail to be seen
not a sound to be heard
nothing

nothing at all.

Unless that small smudge
on the far horizon
where a black line cuts
the rim of the sky

is moving?

Is it a distant ship
with full sail and pennants
flying from every masthead?

Is that a skull and crossbones
grinning back at me
from the over waves?

Is it?

A selected list of titles available from Macmillan Children's Books

The prices shown below are correct at the time of going to press. However, Macmillan Publishers reserves the right to show new retail prices on covers, which may differ from those previously advertised.

Pirate Stories	978-0-330-45148-2	£4.99
Chosen by Emma Young		
How to Survive School	978-0-330-43951-0	£3.99
Poems chosen by David Harmer		
Spill the Beans	978-0-330-39214-3	£3.99
Poems chosen by David Harmer and Paul Cookson		
Space Poems	978-0-330-44057-8	£3.99
Chosen by Gaby Morgan		
The Truth About Parents	978-0-330-47733-8	£5.99
Poems by Paul Cookson, David Harmer, Brian Moses and Roger Stevens		

All Pan Macmillan titles can be ordered from our website, www.panmacmillan.com, or from your local bookshop and are also available by post from:
Bookpost, PO Box 29, Douglas, Isle of Man IM99 1BQ
Credit cards accepted. For details:
Telephone: 01624 677237
Fax: 01624 670923
Email: bookshop@enterprise.net
www.bookpost.co.uk